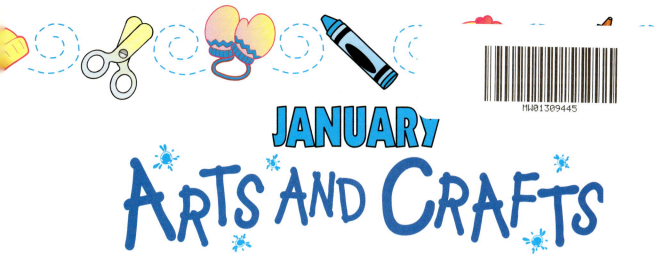

January Arts and Crafts

A MONTH OF ARTS AND CRAFTS AT YOUR FINGERTIPS!

Preschool–Kindergarten

Editors:
Mackie Rhodes
Jan Trautman

Artists:
Pam Crane
Sheila Krill
Rebecca Saunders

Cover Artist:
Kimberly Richard

www.themailbox.com

©2000 by THE EDUCATION CENTER, INC.
All rights reserved.
ISBN10 #1-56234-376-9 • ISBN13 #978-156234-376-7

Except as provided for herein, no part of this publication may be reproduced or transmitted in any form or by any means, electronic or mechanical, including photocopying, recording, or storing in any information storage and retrieval system or electronic online bulletin board, without prior written permission from The Education Center, Inc. Permission is given to the original purchaser to reproduce patterns and reproducibles for individual classroom use only and not for resale or distribution. Reproduction for an entire school or school system is prohibited. Please direct written inquiries to The Education Center, Inc., P.O. Box 9753, Greensboro, NC 27429-0753. The Education Center®, The Mailbox®, and the mailbox/post/grass logo are registered trademarks of The Education Center, Inc. All other brand or product names are trademarks or registered trademarks of their respective companies.

Manufactured in the United States
10 9 8 7 6

Table of Contents

New Year Cheer 3
Ringing Resolutions 4
Balloon Buddy 5
Masquerade Mask 6
Twelve-Month Mural 7
Paper Plate Snowflake 8
Lace-Up Ice Skates 9
Snowpal 10
Snowman Links 11
"Scent-sational" Snowman 12
Snow Measuring Stick 13
Winter Windsock 14
Polar Bear Magnet 15
Winter Rabbit 16
Penguin Pencil Holder 17
Beautiful Bird 18
Peekaboo Bird Feeder 19
Dragon Hand Puppet 20
Magic Wand Pencil Topper 22
Patterns 23

New Year Cheer

Generate New Year enthusiasm with this cheerful craft. Display the completed projects on a festive New Year bulletin board.

Materials (per child)

- construction paper megaphone (page 23)
- New Year poem (page 23)
- curling ribbon
- decorative supplies, such as confetti, glitter, and hole punches
- scissors
- glue
- water-thinned glue (see Teacher Tips)
- paintbrush

Directions

1. Cut out the megaphone and the poem.
2. Glue the poem onto the megaphone.
3. Paint around the text with water-thinned glue and then sprinkle the decorations onto the glue.
4. After the glue dries, glue lengths of curling ribbon to the back of the megaphone.

Teacher Tips

- Mix equal parts of glue and water in a container to make water-thinned glue.
- When the glue is dry, curl each ribbon with scissors.

Mackie Rhodes—Greensboro, NC

Ringing Resolutions

Ring in New Year's resolutions with these adorable door hangers. Invite each child to share his door hanger with the class and then display it at home as a ringing resolution reminder.

Materials (per child)

- construction paper door hanger (page 24)
- two 12" lengths of ribbon
- egg cup
- jingle bell
- aluminum foil
- pencil
- scissors
- crayons
- hole puncher

Directions

1. Cut out the door hanger pattern. Punch holes in the cutout where indicated.
2. Write and illustrate a resolution on the cutout and then sign your name.
3. Tie a length of ribbon to the holes at the top of the door hanger.
4. Mold a piece of aluminum foil around the egg cup so that it resembles a bell.
5. Use the pencil to poke a hole in the bottom of the egg cup.
6. Thread a length of ribbon through the jingle bell loop. Then thread both ends through the hole in the foil bell.
7. Lace the bell ribbon through the bottom hole of the door hanger; then tie the loose ends of the ribbon into a bow.

Teacher Tips
- To keep the foil intact, tape or glue the ends of the foil inside the egg cup.
- For durability, back each hole in the door hanger with a hole reinforcer.
- If desired, laminate the door hanger before attaching the bell and the ribbon.

adapted from an idea by Sue DeRiso—Barrington, RI

Balloon Buddy

Invite these colorful guys to hang around your classroom for your New Year festivities.

Materials (per child)
- text pattern (page 25)
- hand, foot, and mouth tracers—optional (see Teacher Tips)
- 12" half-circle tagboard tracer
- 9" round balloon
- two 1" x 9" construction paper strips (legs)
- two 1" x 3" construction paper strips (arms)
- assorted construction paper colors
- 2 wiggle eyes
- craft glue
- clear tape
- scissors
- yarn
- hole puncher
- pencil

Directions
1. Trace the half circle onto the paper color of your choice.
2. Also trace or draw two hands, two feet, and a mouth, and cut them out.
3. Cut out the text pattern and glue it onto the half circle as shown. Then shape the half circle into a party hat, taping the ends together.
4. Accordion-fold the arm and leg strips and tape each one to the balloon.
5. Glue on the hand and foot cutouts.
6. Glue the wiggle eyes and the mouth onto the balloon.
7. Punch a hole in the top of the hat (through two thicknesses of paper). Lace a length of yarn through the holes and tie the ends together to create a hanger for the balloon buddy.

Teacher Tips
- If you choose to use tracers, make them by cutting out tagboard copies of the hand, foot, and mouth patterns on page 25.
- In advance, solicit the help of adult volunteers to inflate a class supply of balloons.

(**Note:** Since balloons can be choking hazards for small children, supervise children closely during this activity.)

Sue DeRiso—Barrington, RI

Masquerade Mask

Who's behind that mask? Inquiring minds will want to know! Invite youngsters to parade behind these creative masks during your New Year celebrations.

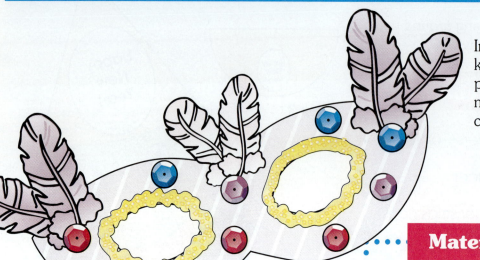

Materials (per child)

- mask tracer (see Teacher Tips)
- poster board
- wrapping paper (optional)
- craft items, such as sequins, feathers, jewels, glitter, and ribbon
- wide craft stick
- scissors
- craft knife (for adult use)
- glue
- markers
- pencil

Teacher Tips

- Cut out tagboard copies of the mask pattern on page 26 to use as tracers.
- Depending on your students' cutting abilities, you might prefer to cut out a mask for each child ahead of time.

Directions

1. Trace the mask onto poster board; then cut out the outline. Have an adult cut out the eyeholes with a craft knife.
2. If desired, trace the mask onto wrapping paper, cut out the mask and eyeholes, and then glue the wrapping paper mask onto the poster board cutout.
3. Decorate the mask with the craft items of your choice.
4. Glue a craft stick to one side of the mask.

Margaret Southard—Cleveland, NY

Twelve-Month Mural

Use this simple mural to help each child associate the months of the year with special celebrations and events.

Materials (per child)

- copy of mural patterns (page 27)
- 2 sentence strips
- clear tape
- crayons
- seasonal stickers and/or stamps (optional)
- scissors
- glue

Directions

1. Tape the two sentence strips together to create one long strip.
2. Fold the long strip in half. Then fold it into thirds and then in half again. Unfold the strip to reveal 12 sections.
3. Cut apart each month label and mural picture. Then pair each month with the corresponding picture.
4. Sequence and glue each label-and-picture pair onto a separate section of the sentence strip.
5. After the glue dries, color each picture; then add your own art to each section. Or add a sticker or stamp that represents a special occasion celebrated during that month.

Margaret Southard—Cleveland, NY

Teacher Tips

- If desired, laminate each child's mural for durability.
- As an alternative, students might cut out a small magazine picture to represent each month and then glue it onto the corresponding section.

Paper Plate Snowflake

Let it snow! Display these beautiful paper plate snowflakes with a wishful snowy title and youngsters will be eager to share their snow wishes with each other. Little ones just can't get enough of that wonderful white fluff!

Materials (per child)
9" blue paper plate (or blue construction paper circle)
snowflake-shaped sponge
white tempera paint
silver glitter
silver ribbon
hole puncher
glue

Directions
1. Sponge-paint white snowflakes onto the plate. Allow the paint to dry.
2. Draw glue designs around the edge of the plate; then sprinkle glitter onto the glue.
3. When the glue is dry, punch evenly spaced holes around the plate rim. Then lace the ribbon through the holes.
4. Tie the ends of the ribbon into a bow.

Teacher Tips
- If blue paper plates are not available, you could use a construction paper circle or have each child paint a white paper plate blue.
- For home display purposes, attach a piece of magnetic tape or hot-glue a ribbon loop to the back of each child's paper plate.

adapted from an idea by Julie A. Koczur—VAFB, CA

Lace-Up Ice Skates

Youngsters will glide right into lacing and tying practice when they create these unique ice skates.

Materials (per child)

- skate tracer (see Teacher Tips)
- construction paper
- 2 wide craft sticks
- two 30" lengths of yarn
- 10" length of yarn
- 10 hole reinforcers
- paint pens
- scissors
- glue
- hole puncher
- chalk and hairspray (optional)

Directions

1. Trace the skate tracer twice onto construction paper. Mark each of the holes. Cut out each shape and then punch out the holes where indicated.
2. Affix a hole reinforcer over each of the five holes along the front of one skate cutout.
3. Flip the second cutout and repeat Step 2 for this skate. When you finish, you will have a left and a right skate.
4. Decorate each skate with paint pens.
5. Glue a craft stick onto the bottom of each skate to resemble a blade.
6. Lace each skate—in crisscross fashion—with a 30" length of yarn and then tie the ends of the yarn into a bow.
7. Punch a hole in the top corner of each skate and tie the skates together with the 10" length of yarn.

Susan Bunyan—Dodge City, KS

Teacher Tips

- To make a tracer, cut out a tagboard copy of the skate pattern on page 28; then punch holes in the skate where indicated.
- If desired, have students decorate their skates with chalk; then spray each skate with hairspray.
- For durability, laminate each child's decorated skates; then have him use craft glue to glue on the craft stick.

Snowpal

This jolly fellow is quite a little "carrot-ter"! Display these special snowpals around your classroom to spread cheer to youngsters throughout the day.

Materials (per child)

- hat, mitten, and boot tracers (see Teacher Tips)
- small white paper plate
- large white paper plate
- black construction paper
- orange bumpy chenille section
- buttons
- 15" length of ribbon
- wrapping paper
- markers
- scissors
- glue
- tape
- hole puncher

Directions

1. Trace the hat once and the boot twice onto black construction paper. Then trace the mitten twice onto a piece of wrapping paper. Cut out all the shapes.
2. Glue the hat onto the small plate to create the snowpal's head.
3. Draw eyes and a mouth on the face; then poke one end of the chenille piece through the plate to represent a carrot nose. Bend and tape the inserted end to the back of the head.
4. To make the body, glue the mittens and boots onto the large paper plate as shown. Then glue buttons onto the body.
5. After the glue dries, punch a hole near the bottom of the head and one near the top of the body. Tie the two sections together with the ribbon.

Teacher Tips
- To make tracers, cut out a tagboard copy of the hat, mitten, and boot patterns on page 29.
- To eliminate the sharp point at the end of the chenille nose, fold the tip back onto itself.

Susan Bunyan—Dodge City, KS

Snowman Links

Link the indoors with the outdoors by displaying these paper-chain snowmen in your classroom windows.

Materials (per child)
- hat and scarf tracer (see Teacher Tips)
- three 2" x 11" strips of white construction paper
- construction paper scraps
- sandpaper scraps
- 2 wiggle eyes
- 3 small pom-poms
- ribbon
- scissors
- glue
- hole puncher

Directions
1. Glue the ends of one paper strip together to form a loop. Repeat with the second and third strips, linking the loops together to create a paper chain.
2. Trace the hat and scarf onto construction paper; then cut out each shape.
3. Cut out a construction paper nose and punch several holes from colored paper for the mouth.
4. Glue all the cutouts and the wiggle eyes onto the top chain link (as shown).
5. Cut out and glue sandpaper arms onto opposite sides of the middle link and fold them forward.
6. Glue the pom-poms on the bottom link.
7. After the glue dries, loop a ribbon hanger through the top link.

Teacher Tips
- To make tracers, cut out a tagboard copy of the hat and scarf patterns on page 26.
- Secure the ribbon hanger inside the top link with a piece of tape.
- Put a piece of rolled tape between each snowman link to hold it in place.
- Invite children to make different sizes of snowpeople!

Kimberli Carrier—Nashua, NH

"Scent-sational" Snowman

These scented snowmen are fun to make and they sure smell great! To use for a movement activity, invite each child to dance his snowman to the tune of "Frosty, the Snowman" or another seasonal song.

back view

Materials (per child)
- toilet paper tube (cut into thirds)
- short twig (about 5" long)
- white paper
- cotton
- 2 wiggle eyes
- small bead
- short piece of pipe cleaner
- 3 whole cloves
- 23" length of yarn
- construction paper scraps
- tape
- pencil
- fabric scraps
- glue
- scissors
- hole puncher

Directions
1. Trace the round end of a tube three times onto white paper. Cut out each circle a little larger than the outline.
2. Glue each circle onto one end of a different tube section.
3. Punch holes in each tube as shown.
4. Fold the yarn in half and knot it about $3\tfrac{1}{2}$" from the fold. String it through the tubes as shown. Secure with tape.
5. Cut out a paper hat, mittens, and a fabric scarf.
6. Glue cotton onto each circle on the snowman. Add the hat, wiggle eyes, bead nose, pipe cleaner mouth, fabric scarf, and clove buttons.
7. Slide the twig through the two side holes. Put a dot of glue in each hole to hold the twig in place; then glue a mitten onto each end of the twig.

Teacher Tips
- If white toilet paper tubes are not available, have each child paint a tube with white tempera paint.
- Take youngsters on a wintry nature walk to find the twigs for their snowmen's arms.
- If desired, as a last step, glue cotton into the back of each tube to cover the yarn.

Susan DeRiso—Barrington, RI

Snow Measuring Stick

How deep is the snow on the ground? Or the snow substitute in the sensory table? How tall are my snow boots? How long is my mitten? Invite each child to use this special measuring stick to discover the answers to these questions and more.

Materials (per child)

- 1' wooden paint stirrer
- black felt
- 1/2" x 8" strip of flannel
- 2 wiggle eyes
- small black pom-pom
- white tempera paint
- black permanent marker
- scissors
- paintbrush
- glue
- ruler

Directions

1. Paint the wooden stirrer white; then set it aside to dry.
2. Cut out a black felt hat and glue it onto the handled end of the stick.
3. Glue the wiggle eyes and pom-pom nose onto the stick to create a snowman's face.
4. Cut small snips of felt; then glue them onto the face to represent a mouth.
5. Tie the flannel strip (scarf) around the contoured section of the stick.
6. Starting at the bottom, use the marker and a ruler to mark eight one-inch increments on the stick.
7. Label the back of the stick with "Let It Snow!" and the artist's name.

Teacher Tips

- If desired, put a dot of glue under the scarf to hold it in place.
- To use the full length of the stick for measuring items, label the front with "Let It Snow!"; then label one-inch increments from 1 to 12 on the back.

Sue DeRiso—Barrington, RI

Winter Windsock

Capture the essence of winter with this cool seasonal windsock. Suspend each child's creation from your classroom ceiling for an interesting display. Or have her take her windsock home to share with her family.

Materials (per child)
- assortment of snowflake stencils (see Teacher Tips)
- large sheet of white construction paper
- 1½" x 18" strip of light blue construction paper
- light blue paint
- six 4" white doilies
- six 12" white streamers
- sponge
- scissors
- tape
- stapler

Directions
1. Use small pieces of rolled tape to secure several snowflakes to the white paper.
2. Sponge blue paint over the snowflakes and the entire surface of the paper.
3. Carefully remove the snowflakes from the paper; then allow the paint to dry.
4. Staple the ends of the painted paper together to create a tube.
5. Fold each doily into fourths; then snip out small shapes from the tip and the folded and rounded edges. Be sure not to cut off an entire folded edge.
6. Unfold each doily to reveal a unique snowflake. Staple each snowflake onto the end of a separate streamer.
7. Staple the streamers at even intervals along one end of the tube.
8. Staple the blue paper strip to the opposite end of the tube to make a handle for the windsock.

adapted from an idea by Sue DeRiso—Barrington, RI

Teacher Tips
- To make snowflake stencils, laminate a supply of tagboard. Then die-cut snowflakes from the laminated tagboard.

Polar Bear Magnet

Chill out with this friendly polar bear magnet. Encourage each child to take his magnet home to display on his family's refrigerator or any other magnetic surface.

Materials (per child)
- juice can lid (or canning jar lid)
- cotton balls
- 2 wiggle eyes
- black pom-pom
- about 2" of black pipe cleaner
- magnetic tape
- glue

Directions
1. Gently stretch out several cotton balls; then glue them onto the lid to create the bear's head.
2. To make ears, glue two cotton balls at the top of the head.
3. For the bear's snout, glue two cotton balls side by side in the center of the head.
4. Glue wiggle eyes, a pom-pom nose, and a pipe cleaner mouth onto the head.
5. After the glue dries, attach magnetic tape to the back of the bear.

Teacher Tips
- Shape the pipe cleaner mouth into a wide W; then glue it onto the head.
- If desired, lightly dab the center of each ear with red watercolor paint or a pink marker.

Margaret Southard—Cleveland, NY

Winter Rabbit

Every "bunny" in your class will enjoy creating these snow bunny pictures. Display these pictures on a bulletin board covered with quilt batting to enhance the wintry feel.

Materials (per child)
- rabbit tracer (see Teacher Tips)
- half sheet of construction paper (in a bunny color)
- blue construction paper
- cotton balls
- iridescent glitter
- small branchy twig
- white chalk or crayon
- scissors
- water-thinned glue
- paintbrush
- glue

Directions
1. Glue a row of cotton balls along the bottom edge of the paper to represent a snow-covered ground.
2. Use chalk to outline the rabbit tracer on the half sheet of construction paper. Cut out the rabbit; then glue it on the snow-covered ground.
3. Glue the twig along one side of the paper so that it resembles a tree or bush.
4. To make snowflakes, use scissors to snip a cotton ball into small pieces. Fluff each snowflake.
5. Paint water-thinned glue over the entire picture; then lightly sprinkle the cotton snowflakes and glitter onto the glue to create a wintry scene.

Mackie Rhodes—Greensboro, NC

Teacher Tips
- To make a tracer, cut out a tagboard copy of the rabbit pattern on page 30.
- To make water-thinned glue, mix equal amounts of glue and water.
- In advance, bundle youngsters up and take them on a winter nature walk to collect twigs for this activity.

Penguin Pencil Holder

Pencils, markers, and rulers will find a cozy resting place in this personalized penguin pencil holder. When the utensils are not in use, have each child store her pencil holder in a designated area in the classroom to create a penguin rookery.

Materials (per child)

- penguin wing, beak, bow, and tie tracers (see Teacher Tips)
- plastic barrel-shaped canister (from powdered soft drink mix)
- black and orange construction paper
- foil wrapping paper
- 2 wiggle eyes
- black tempera paint (see Teacher Tips)
- white chalk
- permanent marker
- scissors
- craft glue
- paintbrush

Directions

1. Paint the top portion of the canister black and let it dry.
2. Using chalk, outline the wing tracer twice onto black paper; then trace the beak onto orange paper and the bow or tie onto a piece of wrapping paper. Cut out each shape.
3. Use the marker to personalize the bow (or tie).
4. Glue on the eyes, wings, beak, and bow (or tie) as shown.
5. After the glue dries, fold the beak so that it points out.
6. Fill the penguin pencil holder with pencils, markers, rulers, and other utensils of similar length.

Teacher Tips

- To make tracers, cut out tagboard copies of the wing, beak, bow, and tie patterns on page 30.
- Add a few drops of dishwashing liquid to the paint. This will prevent it from peeling off the canister.

Beautiful Bird

Convert a simple paper plate into a beautiful bird! Then display these lovely creatures to cheer up the winter scenery in your classroom.

Materials (per child)

- bird tracer (see Teacher Tips)
- 9" white paper plate
- blue, brown, or red tempera paint
- gray tempera paint
- 2 wiggle eyes
- ribbon
- newspaper
- marker
- scissors
- glue
- paintbrush

Directions

1. Paint the front of the plate with the color of your choice; then set it aside to dry.
2. Turn the plate over and then paint the back of the plate with the same color.
3. Crumple a piece of newspaper into a loose ball. Dip the ball into gray paint and lightly blot the front of the plate with it. Let it dry.
4. Turn the plate over and repeat Step 3.
5. After the paint dries, fold the plate in half toward the back. Fit the bird tracer to the folded plate as shown; then trace it onto the plate.
6. Cut out the bird outline through both thicknesses of the plate.
7. Glue the head and body sections together (as shown), leaving the wings and tail free. Insert a loop of ribbon into the glue as shown.
8. Glue a wiggle eye to each side of the head.
9. After the glue dries, spread the wings and tail so that the bird appears to be flying.

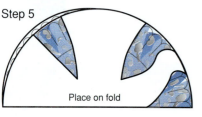

Step 5 — Place on fold

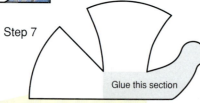

Step 7 — Glue this section

Teacher Tips

- Cut out a tagboard copy of the bird pattern on page 31 to make a tracer.
- Clip a clothespin onto the head and body sections to hold them together while the glue dries.
- To make a peace dove, simply blot gray paint onto the white paper plate; then follow Steps 5–9.

Mackie Rhodes—Greensboro, NC

Peekaboo Bird Feeder

These see-through feeders give young bird-watchers a clearer view of the birds—and of the seed level inside! Encourage each child to hang his bird feeder in an easy-to-view area outside your classroom (or his home); then let the bird-watching begin!

Materials (per child)

- 9-oz. clear plastic tumbler
- 2½" paper square
- round chopstick
- markers
- paint pens
- ribbon
- hole puncher
- glue
- tape
- birdseed

Directions

1. Draw a simple picture or design on the paper square.
2. Tape the picture inside the cup so that it can be seen from the outside. Trace the picture on the cup with paint pens; then color the design as desired.
3. Remove and tape the picture inside the cup again so that it can be traced (as in Step 2) without overlapping the previous drawing. After tracing and coloring the picture, repeat this process as desired.
4. After the paint dries, punch four equally spaced holes just under the cup rim. To make a hanger, tie the ends of a length of ribbon to two opposite holes.
5. To make a perch, slide the chopstick through the two remaining holes; then put a dot of glue in each hole to hold the stick in place.
6. Fill the bird feeder with birdseed and then hang it on a tree limb outdoors.

Mackie Rhodes—Greensboro, NC

Teacher Tips

- If a round chopstick is not available, use an eight-inch length of a quarter-inch dowel.
- Periodically check the seed level in the bird feeder and replenish the supply as needed.

Dragon Hand Puppet

Invite youngsters to parade these colorful dragon puppets around your school to celebrate the start of a great new year!

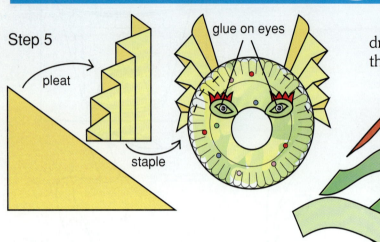

Step 5 — pleat, staple, glue on eyes

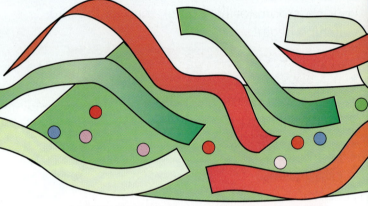

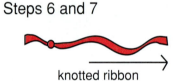

Steps 6 and 7 — knotted ribbon

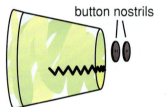

button nostrils

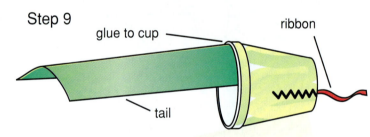

Step 9 — glue to cup, tail, ribbon

Teacher Tips
- To make glue-paint, mix two parts glue with one part tempera paint.
- Use clothespins to hold the tail on the cup while the glue dries.

Materials (per child)

- green construction paper eye patterns (page 32)
- red construction paper eyelash patterns (page 32)
- 8-oz. Styrofoam® cup
- 9" paper plate
- 2 half sheets of green construction paper (cut lengthwise)
- 2 half sheets of yellow construction paper (cut diagonally)
- assorted widths and colors of ribbon and tissue paper strips
- green and yellow glue-paint (see Teacher Tips)
- 2 wiggle eyes
- 2 black buttons
- 3" length of red ribbon
- glitter
- sequins
- permanent marker
- paintbrush
- scissors
- stapler
- glue

Julie Koczur—VAFB, CA

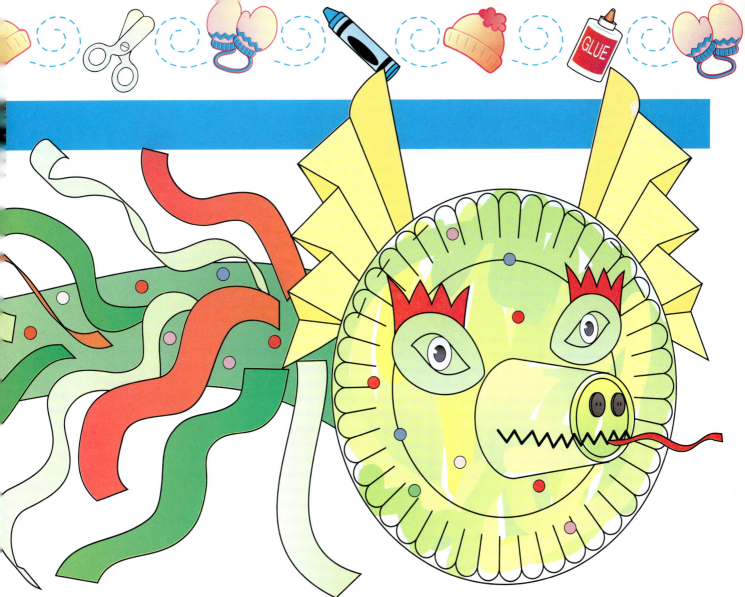

Directions

1. Cut out the eye and eyelash patterns. Glue a wiggle eye and an eyelash onto each eye.
2. To make the head, cut out a three-inch circle from the middle of the plate.
3. Paint the back of the plate with both glue-paint colors. Sprinkle glitter onto the wet paint.
4. After the paint dries on the back, paint and glitter the front of the plate. Add sequins and then press the eyes onto the wet glue. Set the plate aside to dry.
5. Pleat each yellow triangle to create winged ears; then staple each ear onto the plate as shown.
6. Paint and glitter the cup; then press two button nostrils into the wet glue on the bottom of the cup. After the glue dries, draw a mouth on the cup with the marker.
7. Poke a small hole in the bottom of the cup. Knot one end of the red ribbon; then insert the other end through the hole to make a tongue.
8. Tape the green paper halves together to make a long tail strip. Glue ribbon, tissue paper strips, and sequins onto the tail.
9. Glue one end of the tail around the cup rim opposite the button nostrils.
10. Edge the hole in the plate with glue. Fit the cup snugly into the hole; then let the glue dry.

Magic Wand Pencil Topper

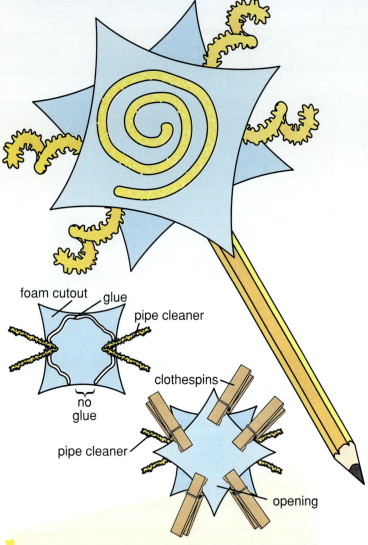

Abracadabra! These special pencil toppers will turn writing into a magical experience for all of your youngsters.

Materials (per child)

- tagboard wand topper tracer (see Teacher Tips)
- craft foam
- gold pipe cleaner
- gold glitter
- scissors
- craft glue
- clothespins
- pencil

Directions

1. Outline the wand topper tracer twice on the craft foam; then cut out both shapes.
2. Cut the pipe cleaner in half. Fold each half to resemble a V.
3. Draw glue lines onto a wand cutout as shown; then position the pipe cleaner Vs on opposite sides of the cutout.
4. Position and press the other wand cutout onto the first one as shown, leaving an opening at the bottom of the shapes. Use clothespins to hold the shapes together while the glue dries.
5. Draw a glue design on the front of the wand; then sprinkle glitter onto the glue.
6. After all the glue dries, curl each pipe cleaner around a pencil.
7. Insert the end of a pencil into the opening; then enter the magical world of writing!

Teacher Tips

- To make tracers, cut out tagboard copies of the wand topper patterns on page 24.
- To eliminate the sharp ends of the pipe cleaners, bend each pipe cleaner tip back onto itself.
- If desired, replace the pencil with a straw; then invite each child to use her magic wand in her dramatic-play activities.

22

Patterns
Use with "New Year Cheer" on page 3.

Hey! Hey!
Give a cheer!
Celebrate
A brand-new year!

_____
(name)

New Year poem

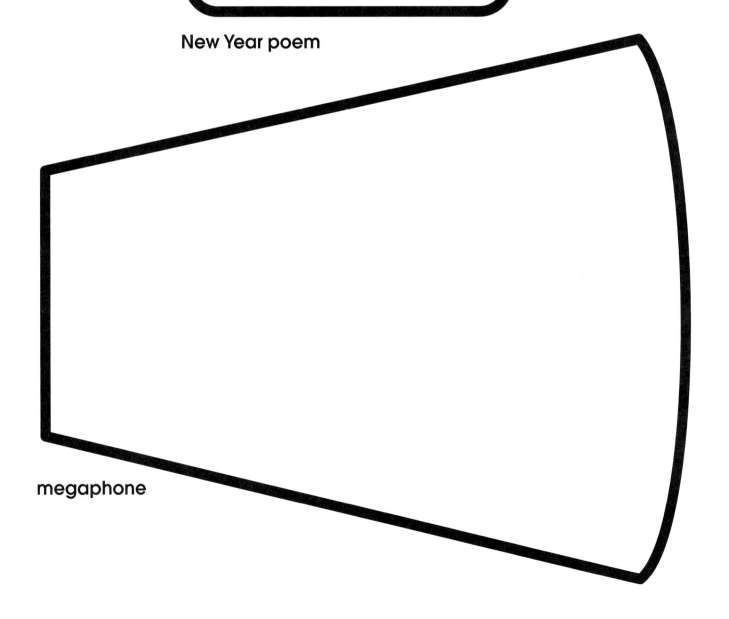

megaphone

©2000 The Education Center, Inc. • *January Monthly Arts and Crafts* • TEC1040

Patterns

Door Hanger
Use with "Ringing Resolutions" on page 4.

Wand Topper
Use with "Magic Wand Pencil Topper" on page 22.

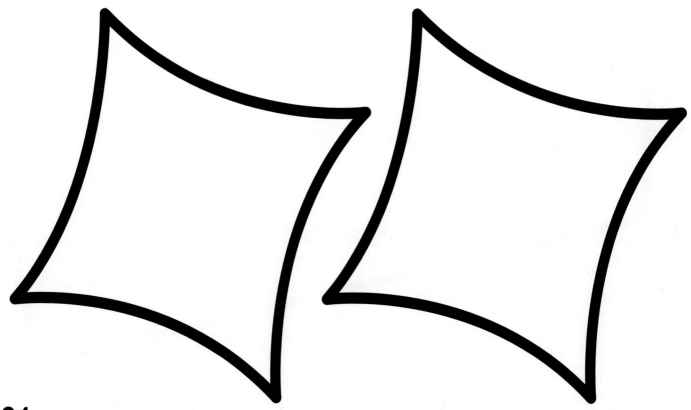

©2000 The Education Center, Inc. • *January Monthly Arts and Crafts* • TEC1040

Balloon Buddy Patterns
Use with "Balloon Buddy" on page 5.

Mask Pattern
Use with "Masquerade Mask" on page 6.

Hat and Scarf Patterns
Use with "Snowman Links" on page 11.

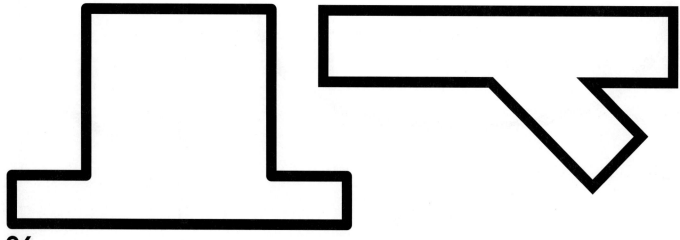

Mural Patterns

Use with "Twelve-Month Mural" on page 7.

Months

January	February	March
April	May	June
July	August	September
October	November	December

Mural pictures

Skate Pattern
Use with "Lace-Up Ice Skates" on page 9.

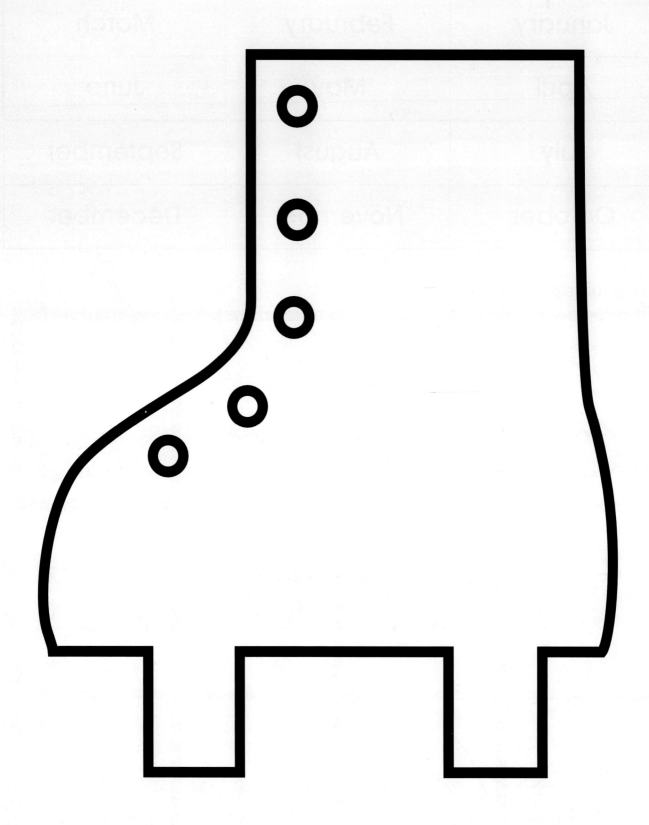

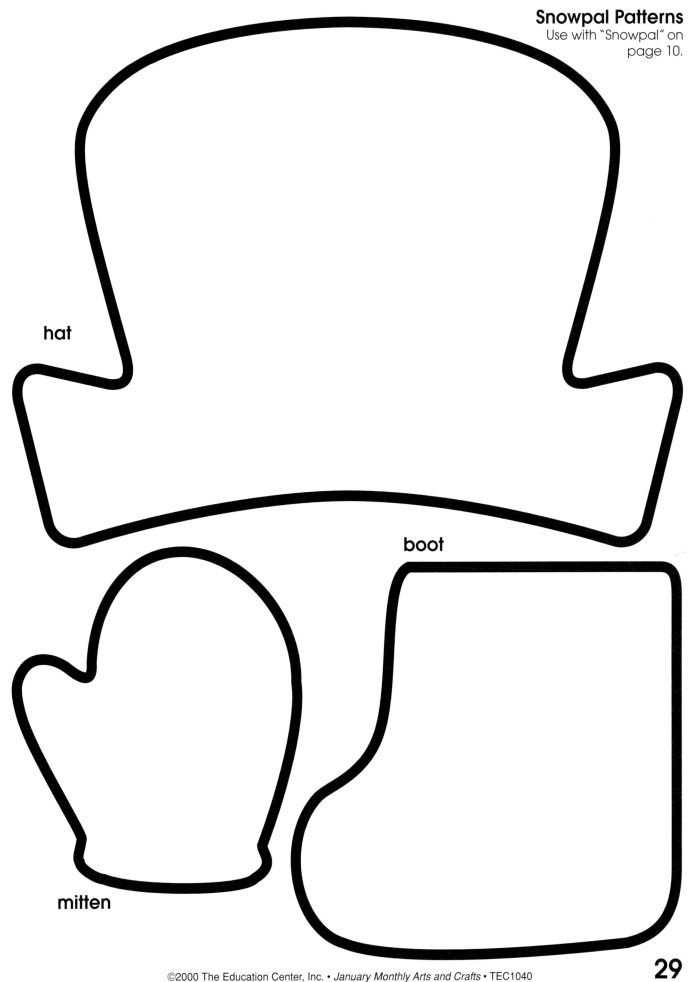

Rabbit Pattern
Use with "Winter Rabbit" on page 16.

Penguin Patterns
Use with "Penguin Pencil Holder" on page 17.

wing

bow

tie

beak

Bird Pattern
Use with "Beautiful Bird" on page 18.

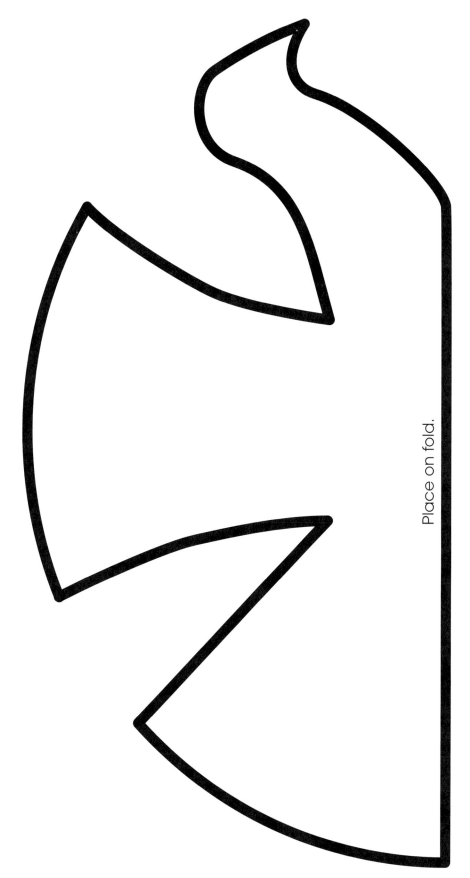

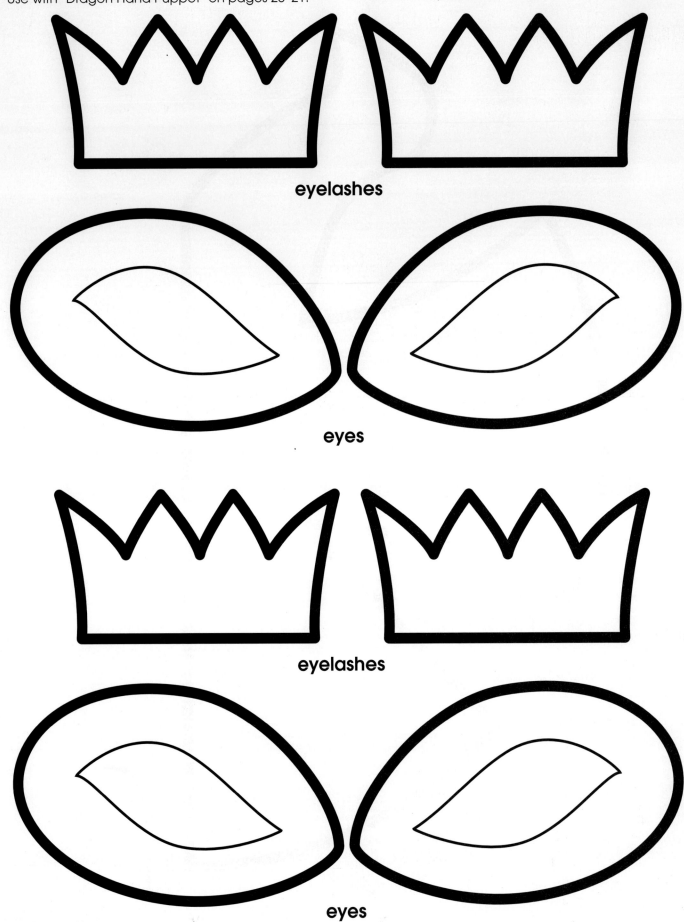